Introduction to the Dictionary

Hi! My name is Library Luke. This is my pal, Info. We are here to introduce you to a very helpful friend. Our helpful friend is a book called a DICTIONARY. A dictionary can help us with many important things. It can help us spell a word correctly. When we have trouble saying a word, the dictionary will help us pronounce it the right way. Dictionaries also tell us the definition or meaning of a word.

Dictionaries are easy to use. They are written in ABC order.

Write your alphabet below:

___ ___ ___ ___ ___ ___ ___ ___ ___ ___ ___ ___ ___

___ ___ ___ ___ ___ ___ ___ ___ ___ ___ ___ ___ ___

Cut and paste.
Put the pictures in ABC Order.

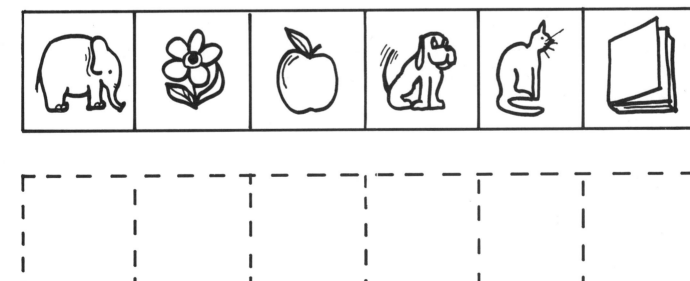

Name_____

ABC Order – I

Poor Info needs to look up a word to get its meaning, but he left his dictionary at home. Find out where Info can look in his Social Studies book to get the meaning he needs by putting these words in alphabetical order and reading the starred letters.

mispronounce   1.   __ __ __ __ __ __
                                *

dilemma   2.   __ __ __ __ __ __ __
                *

balance   3.   __ __ __ __ __ __ __ __ __ __
                *

competitor   4.   __ __ __ __ __ __ __ __
                            *

mysterious   5.   __ __ __ __ __ __
                  *

badger   6.   __ __ __ __ __ __
              *

condense   7.   __ __ __ __ __ __ __ __ __ __ __
                    *

diesel   8.   __ __ __ __ __ __ __ __
          *

The starred letters are _____.

Unscrambled, they spell _____.

ABC Order – II

Luke knows he needs to be good at
ABC order to use the dictionary properly.
Write each missing letter.

_____ comes after K   _____ comes before E
_____ comes after T   _____ comes after H
_____ comes after J   _____ comes after B
_____ comes after D   _____ comes before U
_____ comes before V   _____ comes before J
_____ comes before T   _____ comes before P
_____ comes before F   _____ comes after M
_____ comes ~~before~~ After T   _____ comes before B
_____ comes after S   _____ comes after Q
_____ comes after G   _____ comes after X
_____ comes after D

Write each letter in the order you wrote them above to make a sentence.

J comes after _____   C comes before _____   S comes before _____
M comes before _____   P comes after _____   P comes after _____
G comes after _____   D comes before _____   N comes before _____
N comes before _____   T comes after _____

Write each letter in the order you wrote them above.

ABC Order – III

Info has a problem. He needs help putting these words in ABC order. To put words in ABC order look at the first letter of each word. Use the lines below to put the words in ABC order.

cap	bed	star	pin
foot	ear	x-ray	hair
ice	jacks	owl	under
light	run	ant	you
quit	mouse	whale	goat
zoo	kite	voice	top
nail	doll		

Work across.

_____ _____ _____

_____ _____ _____

_____ _____ _____

_____ _____ _____

_____ _____ _____

_____ _____ _____

_____ _____ _____

_____ _____ _____

Name_____

ABC Order – IV

Luke has noticed that sometimes words start with the same letter. When this happens, look at the second letter in a word.

EXAMPLE: The word **Library** comes before **Luke** in ABC order because **i** comes before **u** in the alphabet.

A B C D E F G H I J K L M N O P Q R S T U V W X Y Z

Put the words in each box in ABC order.

bat	_____	elf	_____
boat	_____	egg	_____
bee	_____	eat	_____
luck	_____	soap	_____
lace	_____	sewn	_____
lock	_____	suit	_____
vice	_____	turkey	_____
voice	_____	teacher	_____
vase	_____	tackle	_____

Library Luke wants you to write the letters of your name in ABC order just for fun!

ABC Order – V

Info wants to help with ABC order. He remembers to look at the first letter of each new word, but he also knows to go to the second letter if the first letters are the same.

Cut out Info's pawprints below. Then paste them in ABC order on page 7. (They will make a funny sentence!)

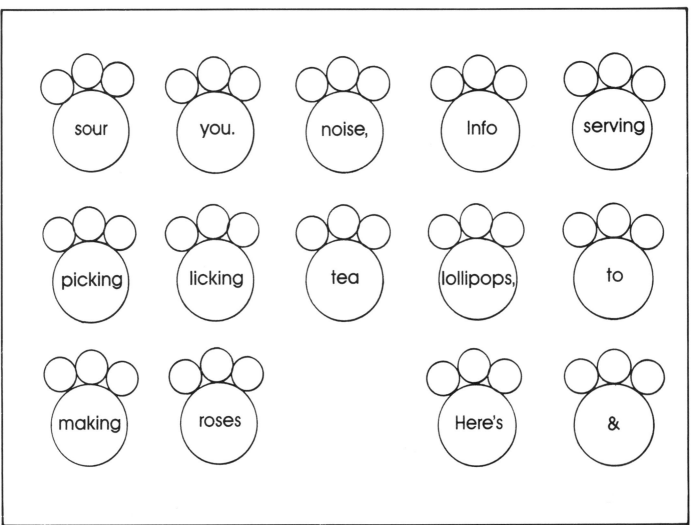

Name_____

ABC Order – V

Paste the pawprints from page 6 in
ABC order below.

Draw a picture to illustrate the silly sentence.

ABC Order – VI

ABC order can get even trickier! Library Luke learned that some words have the same first and second letters. When that happens, look at the third letter of the word.

Practice ABC order on the words below. One box is already in ABC order. Put a red circle around that box.

charm	_____	live	_____
chop	_____	list	_____
cheek	_____	little	_____
child	_____	life	_____

they	_____	post	_____
third	_____	potato	_____
three	_____	porch	_____
thump	_____	pokey	_____

match	_____	jack	_____
mango	_____	jewel	_____
maybe	_____	jade	_____
metal	_____	jelly	_____

ABC Order – VII

Look at Luke's kitchen shelves! Help Luke straighten up by putting each shelf in ABC order.

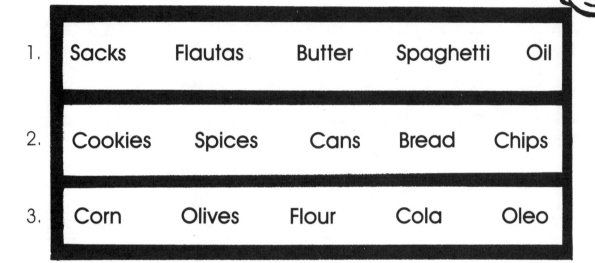

1.	Sacks	Flautas	Butter	Spaghetti	Oil
2.	Cookies	Spices	Cans	Bread	Chips
3.	Corn	Olives	Flour	Cola	Oleo

1.

2.

3.

Write the things in your lunch in ABC order below:

_____   _____

_____   _____

_____   _____

ABC Order – VIII

Info wants your classroom to sit in ABC order. Write the last names of your classmates on the back of this page. Put those names in ABC order on the desks below.

Why Use a Dictionary?

When Mr. Webster first wrote the dictionary, he was doing it so that our writing and spelling could be more standardized.

This standardization is still important, but there are also other reasons that we use the dictionary. Luke had to explain some of these reasons to his assistant, Info.

Why do we use the dictionary?

1. We discover how to spell words.
2. We discover how to pronounce words.
3. We discover what words mean.
4. We discover what part of speech a word is.
5. We discover what the origin of a word is.

Luke also explained to Info that words in a dictionary are always in alphabetical order. To practice this skill, circle the fifth word in each sentence on this page. Then write the words in alphabetical order.

_____   _____   _____

_____   _____   _____

_____   _____   _____

_____   _____   _____

Types of Dictionaries – I

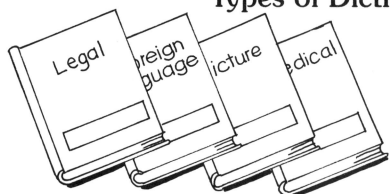

Luke has made a very important discovery. While searching the shelves of the library, he found many types of dictionaries. Use with page 13.

Dictionaries are considered Reference Books. They are books which are not taken from the library. They are used to find meanings and the way to say words.

_____

A Foreign Language Dictionary is a Reference Book used to translate words from one language into another.
EXAMPLE: In an English/Spanish Dictionary the word "hello" would be "hola" in Spanish.

_____

A Picture Dictionary is used by children who do not read. It has pictures to give the meanings of words.

_____

Doctors and nurses use Medical Dictionaries to help them with the words they use everyday.
EXAMPLE: An "immunization" is the medical word for a "shot".

_____

Many other professions have a special dictionary. Can you find another special dictionary in your library? Write the name of it below.

_____

Types of Dictionaries – II

Use page 12 to help you answer the questions below. Then find your answers in the puzzle. The words go across or down.

1. I never leave the library. A dictionary is an example of me. What am I? I am a _____ _____.

2. My language is sometimes different than yours. I translate languages. What am I? I am a _____ _____ Dictionary.

3. I am made up of guide words and definitions. I tell you how to say words too. What am I? I am a _____.

4. I am used by non-readers. What am I? I am a _____ Dictionary.

5. I am helpful to doctors and nurses. What am I? I am a _____ Dictionary.

6. I am helpful to lawyers. I am a _____ Dictionary.

R	F	L	E	G	A	L	G	O	T	O	T
E	O	A	P	H	A	V	E	A	X	P	H
F	R	N	U	H	A	P	P	Y	T	I	E
E	E	G	M	O	D	A	Y	F	V	C	S
R	I	U	D	P	R	S	T	G	R	T	A
E	G	A	L	C	P	B	O	O	B	U	U
N	N	G	B	S	O	R	C	T	R	R	R
C	M	E	D	I	C	A	L	T	S	E	U
E	B	O	O	K	K	M	N	Z	Y	X	S
V	K	S	T	N	E	V	O	T	S	Y	P
O	R	D	I	C	T	I	O	N	A	R	Y

Can you find the secret message in the puzzle?
Write it here._____

Name_____

Types of Dictionaries – III

Info is dressed and ready for a hunt! He wants you to help him find all of the dictionaries you can by searching for the answers to the questions below.

Your Classroom:

1. How many picture dictionaries are in your classroom? _____

   Title:_____

   Publisher:_____

2. What is the title of another dictionary in your classroom?

   _____

3. Look up the word HAPPY and write one definition.

   _____

Your School Library:

1. How many different dictionaries are in your library? _____

   Name two of them:_____

   _____

2. Is there a foreign language dictionary?   yes   no

   What language(s)? _____

   Find the word for HELLO and write it here: _____

Your Home:

1. What is the title of a dictionary in your home?   _____

   _____

2. Write the definition for the word SEEDLING on this line: _____

   _____

3. BONUS: Name any other dictionary you have in your home below:

   _____

   _____

Guide Words – I

GUIDE WORDS are the words at the top of every page in the dictionary. They tell you the first and last word on that page. The word on the left side of the page is the first word on the page. The word on the right side is the last word on the page.

date   dead   dean   down

Help Info by circling the words in **red** that would be found on the left-hand page above. Circle the words in **blue** that would be found on the right-hand page.

deal	daze	data	dead
daunt	decade	deacon	dark
dart	deer	disarm	daub
decal	dip	declare	defect
deceive	decent	degree	drew

Guide Words – II

Circle the words that would be found on these dictionary pages. Remember to use the GUIDE WORDS to help you. Info has already done one for you!

save		seal
(seafood)	sass	sea
seafarer	scene	season
scuba	seam	salt
savage	scurry	say

thirsty		today
thirst	toddle	tiff
toad	time	togs
tissue	third	thumb
thirty	thread	toboggan

what		whet
where	whey	wheezy
whiff	wham	wheel
wheat	wart	wharf
west	whatever	when

Look in your dictionary. Write the GUIDE WORDS at the top of any page you choose. Then list six words you find on that page.

_____   _____

_____   _____   _____

_____   _____   _____

Guide Words – III

Luke has opened his dictionary to two pages. Use the GUIDE WORDS to help you choose the words that belong on the pages.

gremlin	lime	lip	horse
mask	hat	grain	light
litre	most	lost	girl
love	home	hound	matter
man	giraffe	master	ghoul

ghost   house

limb   mat

What words are not found on either page of Luke's dictionary?

_____ _____ _____

Dividing into Syllables

Luke's fourth grade teacher taught Luke a special way to figure how many syllables a word has. This is how Mrs. Moser taught Luke to do it. Put your hand under your chin and say the word. Count the number of times your chin touches your hand. Luke also learned how to identify a word's syllables in a dictionary. Here is an example of a word divided into syllables from a dictionary.

EXAMPLE: Bal ti more

1·2·3

Try the chin/hand method on each of the words and write the number of syllables. Then look and see how the dictionary divides it and copy it.

1. hospital _____

2. window _____

3. fashion _____

4. bandwagon _____

5. reunify _____

6. policy _____

7. department _____

8. Mississippi _____

9. legislate _____

10. snowmobile _____

11. sociology _____

12. zodiac _____

Spelling

Every time Luke gets stuck on a word and can not figure out how to spell it, his teacher tells him to look it up in the dictionary. When this happens, Luke is puzzled and is not sure how to look it up. Below are some steps to follow to help Luke find words he is unsure about.

Spelling......
steps to follow......

Steps:
1. First, decide what the word starts with by saying it to yourself and identifying the beginning letter.
2. Second, decide if the word will be in the front, middle or back of the dictionary.
3. Third, look at the guide words to find ones that you think have the same beginning three letters as the word you are trying to spell.

Now, rewrite these three rules in your own words, and then try them out on three words you cannot spell.

1. _____

2. _____

3. _____

Write the three words you looked up and their definitions.

_____   _____

_____   _____

_____   _____

Name_____

Definitions – I

Help Info find the meaning of the underlined words in the dictionary. Then write TRUE or FALSE before each sentence. Turn your paper over and write a correct sentence for each one that is false.

_____ 1. The diamond was cut into the shape of a <u>baguette</u>.

_____ 2. Donna used a <u>nosegay</u> to keep her nose warm last winter.

_____ 3. Princess Dianna wears a <u>tibia</u> of jewels on her head.

_____ 4. A flooded field where rice is grown is called a <u>paddy</u>.

_____ 5. A pea is an example of a <u>legume</u>.

_____ 6. There is a <u>gorse</u> growing in our front yard.

_____ 7. Please fix the <u>leek</u> in the kitchen sink.

_____ 8. We are serving a <u>brioche</u> with dinner tonight.

_____ 9. Our house is so clean it is in <u>disrepair</u>.

_____ 10. It is an old saying that, "<u>Hindsight</u> is the best sight."

　　　　　　　　IF5071 Library and Reference Skills

Name_____

Definitions – II

Library Luke and his pal, Info, have discovered that some words have more than one meaning. Use the definitions below to decide which meaning goes with each underlined word.

bay: 1. a partly enclosed body of water
      2. a place that sticks out in a wall

duck: 1. water bird with webbed feet
      2. to lower quickly to avoid

mine: 1. a tunnel to extract minerals
      2. indicates possession

_____ Ernie has a favorite toy that is a rubber <u>duck</u>.

_____ My dad found coal in the <u>mine</u>.

_____ When the ball flew toward Janie, I yelled, "<u>Duck</u>!"

_____ We eat breakfast at the table by the <u>bay</u> window.

_____ Those green boots are <u>mine</u>.

_____ The Johnsons went on vacation to San Francisco and had a room by the <u>bay</u>.

Name _____

Word-of-the-Day Calendar

MONDAY'S WORD: _____

Found on page: _____

Definition: _____

_____

Here's how I use it in a sentence: _____

_____

TUESDAY'S WORD: _____

Found on page: _____

Definition: _____

_____

Here's how I use it in a sentence: _____

_____

WEDNESDAY'S WORD: _____

Found on page: _____

Definition: _____

_____

Here's how I use it in a sentence: _____

_____

THURSDAY'S WORD: _____

Found on page: _____

Definition: _____

_____

Here's how I use it in a sentence: _____

_____

FRIDAY'S WORD: _____

Found on page: _____

Definition: _____

_____

Here's how I use it in a sentence: _____

Let's Review!

Name_____

Put these words in ABC order.

halt	prize
hub	player
hall	peewee
hive	praise
hole	pick
host	pox

_____   _____

_____   _____

_____   _____

_____   _____

_____   _____

_____   _____

GUIDE

Using the GUIDE WORDS, write the words below on the correct page. Then rewrite them in ABC order.

hunt   horn   hock   how   hoist   hold   humble   house

★ hoax – hose ★

_____ _____

_____ _____

_____ _____

_____ _____

★ hot – hurl ★

_____ _____

_____ _____

_____ _____

_____ _____

Write T or F.

___ Jeff had a <u>hoagie</u> for lunch.

___ The doctor put some <u>savvy</u> on my cut.

___ Put it in the trash can. Don't <u>liter</u>.

___ The gymnast was so <u>agile</u>.

Name_____

Mystery

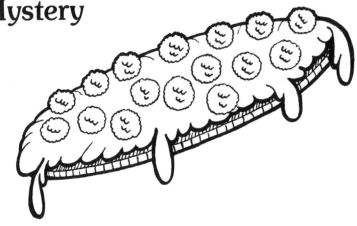

Library Luke and Info have been asked to solve a mystery because they are experts on using the dictionary. They need your help. Solve the clues below after you have read the mystery.

"The Case of the Favorite Pizza"

My friend, Chris, loves to eat pizza. Why, if he had his choice, he would eat it for every meal! The problem is, he is very picky and will only eat one kind of pizza. Tomorrow is his birthday and I want to give him his favorite pizza for a present. It is Luke and Info's job to discover Chris' favorite kind of pizza. Use the clues below to solve this case.

CLUES:

1. Write the word that is the same as "the meanings of".

   _ _ _ _ _ _ _ _ _ _Ⓞ_

2. Luke and Info are experts at using this.

   _ _ _ _ _ _ _Ⓞ_ _

3. How are words organized in the dictionary?

   Ⓞ_ _ _ _ _ _ _ _ _ _ _

4. What words are at the top of each page in the dictionary to help you look up words?

5. Ⓞ_ _ Ⓞ _ _ _ _ _

Write the circled letters below to solve the mystery.

   _ _ U S _ _ _ _

Introduction to Books

Hi! My name is Library Luke. This is my friend Info. Our special new friend is a book. Books can take you to places you have never been before. You can discover amazing facts in books. You can get to know famous people. You can let the imagination of the story take you into make-believe adventures.

Fill in the blanks by using the information you have just read. Then use the letters above each * to answer Luke's Mystery Question at the bottom of the page.

1. The imagination in a book will let you take what kind of an adventure?

   __ __ __ __ - __ __ __ __ __ __ __ __
   　　　　＊

2. Sometimes amazing facts are there for you to do what?

   __ __ __ __ __ __ __ __
   　　　＊

3. You can travel to places you have never what?

   __ __ __ __ __ __ __ __ __ __
   　　　　　　　　＊

4. You may do what with famous people?

   __ __ __ __ __ __ __ __ __
   　　　　　　　＊

5. For Luke these new friends are what? __ __ __ __ __ __ __
   　　　　　　　　　　　　　　　　　　　　＊

MYSTERY QUESTION: What are Luke's new friends? __ __ __ __ __ __

 IF5071 Library and Reference Skills

Name_____

Caring for Books

When Luke started school this September, he was given a brand new reading book to use for the year. His teacher is letting him borrow it. This is what Luke noticed about his new book. It looks sharp, the cover is shiny, and the pages have no pencil marks on them. Boy, is Luke excited! Have you ever borrowed a book from your teacher or the library that is not like the one Luke just got?

Luke has decided that he better follow some rules about taking care of books. Then, when he gives his book back to his teacher in the spring, it will still be in good shape.

Here are his rules:

1. Always make sure your hands are clean when you handle a book.
2. Turn pages carefully.
3. Never write in a book.
4. Keep food, water and pets away from your books.
5. Only mark your place in the book with a bookmark.

Now finish this bookmark at the bottom of the page by writing in one rule you need to remember. Then color and cut out the bookmark on the dotted line.

A RULE TO REMEMBER:

_____

Parts of a Book

Info needs Luke to help him understand some of the important parts of a book.

Spine – One of the first parts of a book you will see is the spine of a book. On the spine you will usually find **Title, Author, Call Numbers** and the **Publishing Company.**

Call Numbers – These numbers on the spine of the book will help you find the book in the library.

Title Page – This is the first page in most books. On this page you will find the **Title, Author** and **Publishing Company.**

Table of Contents – This is usually the second page in a book. On this page you will find the names of all the chapters in the book and the page numbers.

Fill in the blanks.

1. You can find the title of a book on the title page and on the __ __ __ __ __.
   *

2. The spine will have a __ __ __ __ number.
   *

3. The Table of Contents will list each __ __ __ __ __ __ __.
   *

4. The Publishing Company is listed on the spine and the
   __ __ __ __ __ page.
   *

5. To count the chapters look at the __ __ __ __ __ of
   __ __ __ __ __ __ __ __.
   *

spine

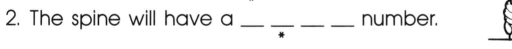

To solve my riddle, fill in the blanks.
I know with your help, Info will say thanks.
He gets mixed up, each time he starts.
Make it clear to him, all the important __ __ __ __ __.

Publishers and Authors

A **Publisher** is a company that produces books.

An **Author** is a person who writes books.

Most of the time the **Publisher** and **Author** of the book are listed on the spine of the book and the title page.

Fill in the blanks.

1. Who is the author of **The Boat**?_____

2. What company published the book?_____

3. What year was the book published?_____

UNSCRAMBLE

I write books. T U O R H A   __ __ __ __ __ __

I produce books. R H P L U B S I E   __ __ __ __ __ __ __ __ __

Illustrator

Do you like to draw pictures? If you do, then someday you may become an **illustrator** of books. An illustrator is a person who draws pictures to go with stories. Just like the author, the illustrator also makes a book come alive. If you like pictures in a book, remember the illustrator's name and watch for other books that he has illustrated.

The illustrator of this book is Dennis Jones. He lives in Elgin, Illinois.

Draw an illustration to go with this book title.

Library Luke Flies to the Moon

Caldecott Medal

Luke has won a special medal. He won this medal for being such a good inspector of mysteries. While Luke was in the library, he found some special books that have won awards. One award is called **The Caldecott Medal**. This award is given each year to the best picture book of the year.

Recent Caldecott Medal Winners

The Glorious Flight: Across the Channel with Louis Bleriot
illustrated by Provensen (1984)
Shadow illustrated by Brown (1983)
Jumanji illustrated by Van Allsburg (1982)

Name a book that you think should earn a special award for art work.

_____

Now draw the medal you will award the illustrator.

Newbery Medal

This special award is given each year to the author that has written the best book for children. Library Luke has found out the Newbery Medal winners in 1983, 1982 and 1981. Can you go to the library or ask your teacher to help you find out the winner in 1984? Put the title on the correct line.

1981 **Jacob Have I Loved** by Paterson

1982 **A Visit to William Blake's Inn** by Willard

1983 **Dicey's Son** by Voight

1984 _____

Now find each of these books in the library. Write one sentence about each book that tells about its cover.

_____

_____

_____

_____

_____

_____

_____

Library ABC Order – I

When putting words in **ABC** order, look at the first letters of the word. Sometimes the first letters in two words are the same. To decide which should come first, look at the second letter of the word.

EXAMPLE: The book **Ramona the Brave** by Beverly Cleary would be placed on the shelf before the book **Pinocchio** by Carlo Collodi because the letter **l** in Cleary comes before the letter **o** in Collodi in the alphabet.

Color me by putting the color words in **ABC** order and following the directions.

orange   yellow   blue   purple   red   black   green   brown

Color my shoes_____.

Color my pants_____.

Color my hair_____.

Color my shirt_____.

Color my thinking cap_____.

Color my backpack_____.

Color my star_____.

Color my lightbulb on my cap_____.

Library ABC Order – II

Luke found out that he had to be pretty good at his **ABC** order if he wanted to find books in the library. To practice, he took his special equipment and placed it in boxes in **ABC** order.

Help Luke by cutting out the pictures and pasting them in the correct boxes in ABC order.

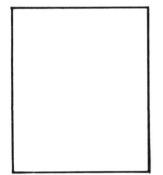

- -

hat

library card

magnifying glass

backpack

Library ABC Order – III

Put these author's last names in **ABC** order and find out what Info's favorite fiction book is. Then write the title of Info's favorite book at the bottom of the page.

AUTHORS

1. __ __ __ __ __ __
      *

2. __ __ __ __ __ __
      *

3. __ __ __ __ __ __ __
         *

4. __ __ __
       *

and

5. __ __ __ __ __ __ __
            *

6. __ __ __ __ __ __ __ __
        *

7. __ __ __ __
      *

8. __ __ __ __
       *

9. __ __ __ __ __ __
         *

10. __ __ __ __ __ __
        *

11. __ __ __ __ __
      *

12. __ __ __
       *

Carolyn Bailey

Ruth Smith

Laurence Yep

Irene Hunt

Maurice Sendak

Berniece Freschet

Beatrix Potter

Joseph Gaer

Elizabeth Enright

Cecil Lewis Day

Rebecca Caudill

Louisa May Alcott

Fiction Books

Luke and Info would like you to meet another one of their friends. His name is Fiction Finch. He is a bird. He is not an ordinary bird. He wears glasses. A real bird would not wear glasses. He is make-believe. That is why his name is Fiction Finch.

A Fiction Book is make-believe too. So, to help you remember what **fiction** means, think of Fiction Finch and his make-believe glasses.

You can find fiction books in the library in **ABC** order using the last name of the author.

Help Fiction Finch put these books in the order you would find them on the shelf of the library. Draw a line from each position to the book title.

Peter Pan by Barrie	1st
The Borrowers by Norton	2nd
Winnie-the-Pooh by Milne	3rd
Fairy Tales by Anderson	4th
Ralph Mouse by Cleary	5th
Charlotte's Web by White	6th
The Cat in the Hat by Seuss	7th
The Biggest Bear by Ward	8th
A Christmas Carol by Dickens	9th
Tom Sawyer by Twain	10th

Non-Fiction Books

Info, Luke and Fiction Finch are going to bake a cake for their favorite librarian who helps them at the library. They need a book that will show them **how to** bake cakes. "How to" books are also called **Non-Fiction**. They are not make-believe, they are true.

Circle the book titles that are Non-Fiction.

The Cat in the Hat	Treasure Island
Building a Doghouse	The Ugly Duckling
History of Baseball	Where the Wild Things Are
How to Make Doll Clothes	Alice in Wonderland
Peter Rabbit	The Incredible Journey
Animals in the Jungle	Abe Lincoln

Now use your crayons to decorate Luke's cake!

Dewey Decimal System

A long time ago a librarian named Dewey invented a way to number books in a library so that they can easily be found.

Luke and Info use the Dewey Decimal System to help them find their favorite books. They learned that books about the same kinds of subjects have the same call numbers on the spines.

To find a Non-Fiction book in the library you use the Dewey Decimal System.

Luke has listed a few of his favorite subjects to look up. He has also listed the call numbers for each subject.

Science – call numbers **500** to **599**

Pets – call numbers **600** to **699**

Sports – call numbers **700** to **799**

Write the correct call numbers next to each book title.

Feeding Your Dog by Owens _____ to _____

Lions in Africa by Downs _____ to _____

Game of Football by Bond _____ to _____

Sports and Games by Kieth _____ to _____

Baseball by Siebert and Vogel _____ to _____

Here Come the Dolphins by Goudey _____ to _____

Canada Geese by Scott _____ to _____

In the Days of the Dinosaurs by Andrews _____ to _____

Picture Books

Each night before Info goes to bed, he likes Luke to read him a story. His favorite kind of books are called picture books because they have a lot of pictures. To find these in the library, Luke uses the Dewey Decimal System. On the picture books Mr. Dewey put a letter **E** and then the first three letters of the author's last name. On the shelves these books are then put in **ABC** order.

Cut these call numbers out on the dotted lines and paste them in the order they would be found on the shelf.

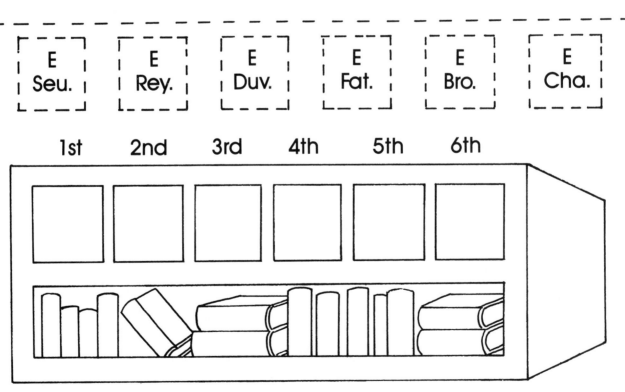

E Seu.	E Rey.	E Duv.	E Fat.	E Bro.	E Cha.

| 1st | 2nd | 3rd | 4th | 5th | 6th |

Biography

Did you know that Thomas Edison invented the electric lightbulb?

Michael Jackson used to sing with his brothers. Do you know how many brothers he sang with?

Library Luke learned about these two famous people when he read their biographies. A biography is a book that tells about the life of a famous person. Luke discovered that biographies are in the library in a special order. Each biography will have the number **92** and the first three letters of the famous person's last name.

Match the call numbers with the famous person's name. The first one has been done for you.

92 Cha	Abraham Lincoln
92 Kin	Harriet Tubman
92 Lee	Daniel Boone
92 Boo	Martin Luther King
92 Ber	Alexander G. Bell
92 Ken	Wilt Chamberlin
92 Kel	Helen Keller
92 Bel	Robert E. Lee
92 Tub	John F. Kennedy
92 Lin	Leonard Bernstein

Poetry

Roses are red,
Tulips are great.
Info is hungry.
For his food,
He can't wait.

Info is writing a book of poetry. When he gets finished, the librarian will put a Dewey Decimal number on the spine of the book. All poetry books have numbers from **800** to **899** and the first three letters of the author's last name. Since Mashun is Info's last name, he will have $\frac{810}{MAS}$ on the spine.

Now circle the call numbers below that you would find on poetry books.

845 Del	760 Tob	370 Mil
257 Nas	345 Kop	390 Wes
500 Del	830 Par	879 Rop
893 Jin	235 Kin	899 Fis
568 Dun	834 Mos	390 End

Cut and Paste Review

Luke has to answer these questions about the library. Will you help Luke? Cut the words out at the bottom of the page and paste them in the correct sentences.

1. The ☐ ☐ is given to the best picture book each year.

2. An ☐ is someone who writes a book.

3. Call numbers are listed on the ☐ of the book.

4. Books about make-believe people are called ☐.

5. The person that draws pictures for books is called an ☐.

6. The best story written each year is given an award called the ☐ ☐.

7. Call numbers were invented by ☐.

8. Books about famous people are called ☐.

Newbery	Author
Biographies	Illustrator
Fiction	Caldecott
Medal	Medal
Dewey	Spine

 IF5071 Library and Reference Skills

Crossword Review

Help Info work the crossword puzzle and discover what is under his bucket.

DOWN

1. Books about famous people are called what?

3. Make-believe books are called what?

4. How should you mark your place in a book?

ACROSS

2. Where are the call numbers written?

3. Which is last in **ABC** order: fat, fox, frog or fish?

5. Who writes books?

Wordsearch Review

Info and Luke have been busy trying to find answers to the six questions below. They had them all figured out, then Info slipped and his paw knocked over the board with the letters on it. Now they are all mixed together! Find and circle the answers to the questions in the wordsearch.

1. Mr. Finch wears glasses. What is his first name that reminds us he is make-believe?

2. What should you use to mark your place in a book?

3. Fiction books are placed on the shelf in **ABC** order using whose last name?

4. What does an illustrator do?

5. What will you find listed by pages in a Table of Contents?

6. What part of the book do you see when you look on a library shelf?

```
P  S  F  L  T  O  M  R  G  S
T  U  I  C  H  A  P  T  E  R
M  U  C  D  A  U  T  H  O  R
L  E  T  O  S  P  D  H  A  R
S  P  I  N  E  T  R  B  N  X
L  B  O  O  K  M  A  R  K  Z
M  W  N  Q  A  T  W  T  D  C
```

Answer Key

Library and Reference Skills

Grades 2 - 3

Page 1

ABC Order

Poor Info needs to look up a word to get its meaning, but he left his dictionary at home. Find out where Info can look in his Social Studies book to get the meaning he needs by putting these words in alphabetical order and reading the starred letters.

mispronounce	1.	badger
dilemma	2.	balance
balance	3.	competitor
competitor	4.	condense
mysterious	5.	diesel
badger	6.	dilemma
condense	7.	mispronounce
diesel	8.	mysterious

The starred letters are ___gaosslry___
Unscrambled, they spell ___glossary___.

Page 2

ABC Order

Luke knows he needs to be good at ABC order to use the dictionary properly. Practice with the puzzles below. The letters you find will tell about the pictures.

L comes after K	D comes before E
U comes after T	I comes after H
K comes after J	C comes after B
E comes after D	T comes before U
U comes before V	I comes before U
S comes before T	O comes before P
E comes before F	N comes after M
S comes before T	A comes before B
T comes after S	R comes after Q
H comes after G	Y comes after X
E comes after D	

Write the answer below.
___Luke uses the dictionary.___

J comes after I	C comes before D	S comes before T
M comes before N	P comes after O	P comes after O
G comes after F	D comes before E	N comes before O
N comes before O	T comes after S	

Write the answer below.
___Info does too.___

Page 3

ABC Order

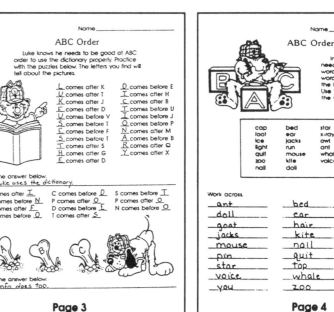

Info has a problem. He needs help putting these words in ABC order. To put words in ABC order look at the first letter of each word. Use the lines below to put the words in ABC order.

cap	bed	star	pin
foot	ear	x-ray	hair
ice	jacks	owl	under
light	run	ant	you
quit	mouse	whale	goat
zoo	kite	voice	top
nail	doll		

Work across.

ant	bed	cap
doll	ear	foot
goat	hair	ice
jacks	kite	light
mouse	nail	owl
pin	quit	run
star	top	under
voice	whale	x-ray
you	zoo	

Page 4

ABC Order

Luke has noticed that sometimes words start with the same letter. When this happens, look at the second letter in a word.

EXAMPLE: The word Library comes before I comes before u in the alphabet.

A B C D E F G H I J K L M N O P Q R S T U V W X Y Z

Put the words in each box in ABC order.

bat	bat	elf	eat
boat	bee	egg	egg
bee	boat	eat	elf
luck	lace	soap	sewn
lace	lock	sewn	soap
lock	luck	suit	suit
vice	vase	turkey	tackle
voice	vice	teacher	teacher
vase	voice	tackle	turkey

Library Luke wants you to write the letters of your name in ABC order just for fun!

Page 5

ABC Order

Info wants to help with ABC order. He remembers to look at the first letter of each new word, but he also knows to go to the second letter if the first letters are the same.

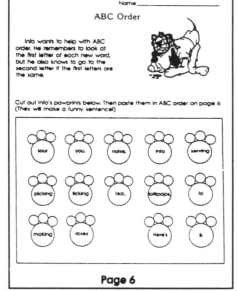

Cut out Info's pawprints below. Then paste them in ABC order on page 6. (They will make a funny sentence!)

Page 6

ABC Order

Paste the pawprints from page 5 in ABC order in the spaces below.

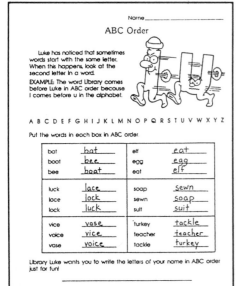

Here's Info licking lollipops, making noise, picking roses & serving sour tea.

Draw a picture to illustrate the silly sentence below.

Page 7

IF5071 Library and Reference Skills

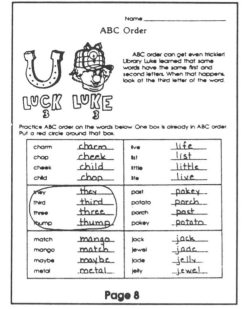

ABC Order

ABC order can get even trickier! Library Luke learned that some words have the same first and second letters. When that happens, look at the third letter of the word.

LUCK LUKE

Practice ABC order on the words below. One box is already in ABC order. Put a red circle around that box.

charm	charm	live	life
chop	cheek	list	list
cheek	child	little	little
child	chop	life	live

they	they	post	pokey
third	third	potato	porch
three	three	porch	post
thump	thump	pokey	potato

match	mango	jack	jack
mango	match	jewel	jade
maybe	maybe	jade	jelly
metal	metal	jelly	jewel

Page 8

ABC Order

Look at Luke's kitchen shelves! What a mess! Help Luke clean up his pantry by putting everything in ABC order.

Socks	Flautas	Butter	Spaghetti	Oil
Cookies	Spices	Cans	Bread	Chips
Corn	Olives	Flour	Cola	Oleo

Bread Butter Cans Chips Cola

Cookies Corn Flautas Flour Oleo

Oil Olives Sacks Spaghetti Spices

Put the things in your lunch in ABC order below.

Page 9

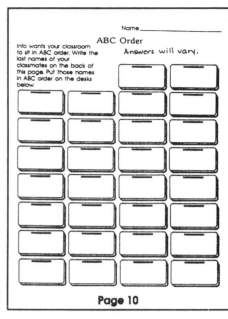

ABC Order

Info wants your classroom to sit in ABC order. Write the last names of your classmates on the back of this page. Put those names in ABC order on the desks below.

Answers will vary.

Page 10

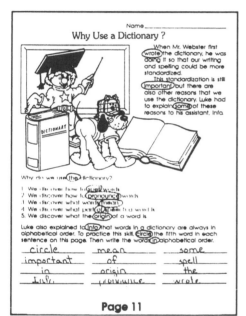

Why Use a Dictionary?

When Mr. Webster first wrote the dictionary, he was doing it so that our writing and spelling could be more standardized.

This standardization is still important, but there are also other reasons that we use the dictionary. Luke had to explain some of these reasons to his assistant, Info.

Why do we use the dictionary?

1. We discover how to spell words.
2. We discover how to pronounce words.
3. We discover what words mean.
4. We discover what part of speech a word is.
5. We discover what the origin of a word is.

Luke also explained to Info that words in a dictionary are always in alphabetical order. To practice this skill, circle the fifth word in each sentence on this page. Then write the words in alphabetical order.

circle	mean	some
important	of	spell
in	origin	the
Info	pronounce	wrote

Page 11

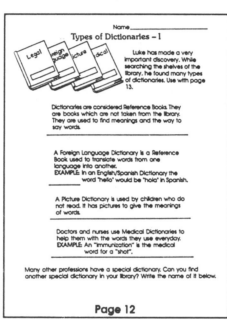

Types of Dictionaries – 1

Luke has made a very important discovery. While searching the shelves of the library, he found many types of dictionaries. Use with page 13.

Dictionaries are considered Reference Books. They are books which are not taken from the library. They are used to find meanings and the way to say words.

A Foreign Language Dictionary is a Reference Book used to translate words from one language into another.
EXAMPLE: In an English/Spanish Dictionary the word "hello" would be "hola" in Spanish.

A Picture Dictionary is used by children who do not read. It has pictures to give the meanings of words.

Doctors and nurses use Medical Dictionaries to help them with the words they use everyday.
EXAMPLE: An "immunization" is the medical word for a "shot".

Many other professions have a special dictionary. Can you find another special dictionary in your library? Write the name of it below.

Page 12

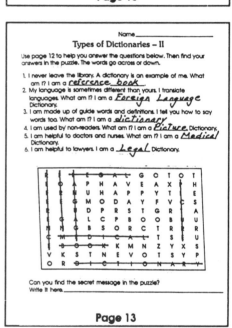

Types of Dictionaries – II

Use page 12 to help you answer the questions below. Then find your answers in the puzzle. The words go across or down.

1. I never leave the library. A dictionary is an example of me. What am I? I am a _reference book_.
2. My language is sometimes different than yours. I translate languages. What am I? I am a _Foreign Language_ Dictionary.
3. I am made up of guide words and definitions. I tell you how to say words too. What am I? I am a _dictionary_.
4. I am used by non-readers. What am I? I am a _Picture_ Dictionary.
5. I am helpful to doctors and nurses. What am I? I am a _Medical_ Dictionary.
6. I am helpful to lawyers. I am a _Legal_ Dictionary.

Can you find the secret message in the puzzle? Write it here.

Page 13

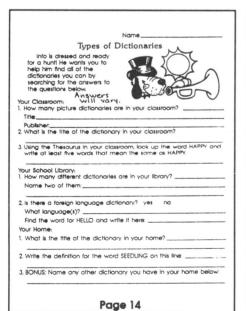

Types of Dictionaries

Info is dressed and ready for a hunt! He wants you to help him find all of the dictionaries you can by searching for the answers to the questions below.

Answers will vary.

Your Classroom:
1. How many picture dictionaries are in your classroom? _____
   Title: _____
   Publisher: _____
2. What is the title of the dictionary in your classroom? _____
3. Using the Thesaurus in your classroom, look up the word HAPPY and write at least five words that mean the same as HAPPY.

Your School Library:
1. How many different dictionaries are in your library? _____
   Name two of them: _____
2. Is there a foreign language dictionary?   yes   no
   What language(s)? _____
   Find the word for HELLO and write it here: _____

Your Home:
1. What is the title of the dictionary in your home? _____
2. Write the definition for the word SEEDLING on this line: _____
3. BONUS: Name any other dictionary you have in your home below.

Page 14

Guide Words

GUIDE WORDS are the words in heavy black letters at the top of every page in the dictionary. They tell you the first and last word on that page. The word on the left side of the page is the first word on the page. The word on the right side is the last word on the page.

date   dead   dean   down

Help Info by circling the words that would be on the above pages.

deal	date	data	dead
daunt	decode	macadam	dark
dart	dear	harm	dough
drool	dle	declare	defect
deceive	decent	degree	drew

Page 15

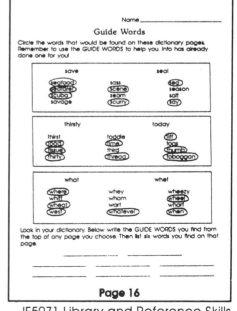

Guide Words

Circle the words that would be found on these dictionary pages. Remember to use the GUIDE WORDS to help you. Info has already done one for you!

save		seal
seafood	sass	sea
saltine	scene	season
scuba	seam	salt
savage	scurry	say

thirsty		today
thirst	toddle	tiff
toads	time	toot
tissue	third	thumb
thirty	thread	toboggan

what		whet
where	whey	wheezy
whiff	wham	wheat
wheat	wart	what
west	whatever	when

Look in your dictionary. Below write the GUIDE WORDS you find from the top of any page you choose. Then list six words you find on that page.

Page 16

Page 17

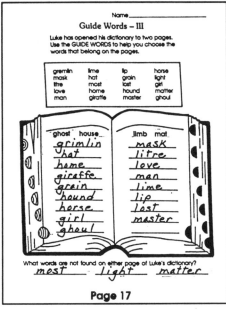

Name_____

Guide Words – III

Luke has opened his dictionary to two pages. Use the GUIDE WORDS to help you choose the words that belong on the pages.

gremlin	lime	lip	horse
mask	hat	grain	light
litre	most	lost	girl
love	home	hound	matter
man	giraffe	master	ghoul

ghost · house	limb · mat
grimlin	mask
hat	litre
home	love
giraffe	man
grain	lime
hound	lip
horse	lost
girl	master
ghoul	

What words are not found on either page of Luke's dictionary?
most   light   matter

Page 17

Page 18

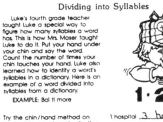

Name_____

Dividing into Syllables

Luke's fourth grade teacher taught Luke a special way to figure how many syllables a word has. This is how Mrs. Moser taught Luke to do it. Put your hand under your chin and say the word. Count the number of times your chin touches your hand. Luke also learned how to identify a word's syllables in a dictionary. Here is an example of a word divided into syllables from a dictionary.

EXAMPLE: Bal·ti·more

Try the chin/hand method on each of the words and write the number of syllables. Then look and see how the dictionary divides it and copy it.

win dow

1. hospital   3   hos·pi·tal
2. window   2   win·dow
3. fashion   2   fash·ion
4. bandwagon   3   band·wag·on
5. reunify   4   re·u·ni·fy
6. policy   3   pol·i·cy
7. department   3   de·part·ment
8. Mississippi   4   Mis·sis·sip·pi
9. legislate   3   leg·is·late
10. snowmobile   3   snow·mo·bile
11. sociology   5   so·ci·ol·o·gy
12. zodiac   3   zo·di·ac

Page 18

Page 19

Name_____

Spelling

Every time Luke gets stuck on a word and can not figure out how to spell it, his teacher tells him to look it up in the dictionary. When this happens, Luke is puzzled and is not sure how to look it up. Below are some steps to follow to help Luke find words he is unsure about.

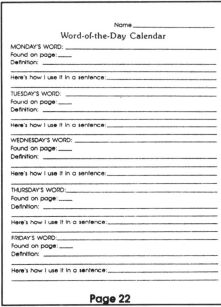

Spelling......
steps to follow......

Steps:
1. First, decide what the word starts with by saying it to yourself and identifying the beginning letter.
2. Second, decide if the word will be in the front, middle or back of the dictionary.
3. Third, look at the guide words to find ones that you think have the same beginning three letters as the word you are trying to spell.

Now, rewrite these three rules in your own words, and then try them out on three words you cannot spell.
1. _____ Answers will vary. _____
2. _____
3. _____

Write the three words you looked up and their definitions.

_____
_____
_____

Page 19

Page 20

Name_____

Definitions

Help Info find the meaning of the underlined words in the dictionary. Then write TRUE or FALSE before each sentence.

TRUE 1. The diamond was cut into the shape of a baguette.
FALSE 2. Donna used a nosegay to keep her nose warm last winter.
FALSE 3. Princess Dianna wears a tibia of jewels on her head.
TRUE 4. A flooded field where rice is grown is called a paddy.
TRUE 5. A pea is an example of a legume.
FALSE 6. There is a gong growing in our front yard.
FALSE 7. Please fix the leek in the kitchen sink.
TRUE 8. We are serving a brioche with dinner tonight.
FALSE 9. Our house is so clean it is in disrepair.
TRUE 10. It is an old saying that, "Hindsight is the best sight."

Page 20

Page 21

Name_____

Definitions

Library Luke and his pal, Info, have discovered that some words have more than one meaning. Use the definitions below to decide which meaning goes with the underlined word.

bay: 1. a partly enclosed body of water
          2. an opening in a wall
duck: 1. water bird with webbed feet
          2. to lower quickly to avoid
mine: 1. a tunnel to extract minerals
          2. indicates possession

1 Ernie has a favorite toy that is a rubber duck.
1 My dad looked cool in the mine.
2 When the ball flew toward Janie, I yelled, "Duck!"
2 We eat breakfast at the table by the bay window.
2 Those green boots are mine.
1 The Johnsons went on vacation to San Francisco and had a room by the bay.

Page 21

Page 22

Name_____

Word-of-the-Day Calendar

MONDAY'S WORD: _____
Found on page: _____
Definition: _____

Here's how I use it in a sentence: _____

TUESDAY'S WORD: _____
Found on page: _____
Definition: _____

Here's how I use it in a sentence: _____

WEDNESDAY'S WORD: _____
Found on page: _____
Definition: _____

Here's how I use it in a sentence: _____

THURSDAY'S WORD: _____
Found on page: _____
Definition: _____

Here's how I use it in a sentence: _____

FRIDAY'S WORD: _____
Found on page: _____
Definition: _____

Here's how I use it in a sentence: _____

Page 22

Page 23

Let's Review!

Name_____

Put these words in ABC order.

halt	prize
hub	player
hall	pewee
hive	praise
hole	pick
host	pox

hall	pewee
halt	pick
hive	player
hole	pox
host	praise
hub	prize

Using the GUIDE WORDS, write the words below on the correct page. Then rewrite them in ABC order.

hunt horn hock how hoist hold humble house

★ hoax - hose ★		★ hot - hurl ★	
horn	hock	hunt	house
hock	hoist	how	how
hoist	hold	humble	humble
hold	horn	house	hunt

Write T or F.
T Jeff had a hoagie for lunch.
F The doctor put some savvy on my cut.
F Put it in the trash can. Don't liter.
T The gymnast was so agile.

Page 23

Page 24

Name_____

Mystery

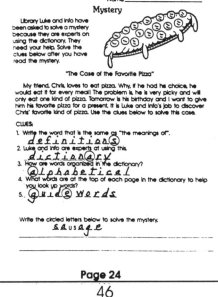

Library Luke and Info have been asked to solve a mystery because they are experts on using the dictionary. They need your help. Solve the clues below after you have read the mystery.

"The Case of the Favorite Pizza"

My friend, Chris, loves to eat pizza. Why, if he had his choice, he would eat it for every meal! The problem is, he is very picky and will only eat one kind of pizza. Tomorrow is his birthday and I want to give him his favorite pizza for a present. It is Luke and Info's job to discover Chris' favorite kind of pizza. Use the clues below to solve this case.

CLUES:
1. Write the word that is the same as "the meanings of".
definition(s)
2. Luke and Info are experts at using this.
dictionary
3. How are words organized in the dictionary?
(a)lphabetical
4. What words are at the top of each page in the dictionary to help you look up words?
g(u)id(e) words

Write the circled letters below to solve the mystery.
sausage
_____

Page 24

Page 25

Name_____

Introduction

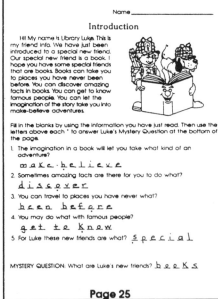

Hi! My name is Library Luke. This is my friend Info. We have just been introduced to a special new friend. Our special new friend is a book. I hope you have some special friends that are books. Books can take you to places you have never been before. You can discover amazing facts in books. You can get to know famous people in books. You can let the imagination of the story take you into make-believe adventures.

Fill in the blanks by using the information you have just read. Then use the letters above each * to answer Luke's Mystery Question at the bottom of the page.

1. The imagination in a book will let you take what kind of an adventure?
make-believe
2. Sometimes amazing facts are there for you to do what?
discover
3. You can travel to places you have never what?
been before
4. You may do what with famous people?
get to know
5. For Luke these new friends are what? special

MYSTERY QUESTION: What are Luke's new friends? books

Page 25

     IF5071 Library and Reference Skills

Caring for Books

When Luke started school this September, he was given a brand new reading book to use for the year. His teacher is letting him borrow it. This is what Luke noticed about his new book. It looks sharp, the cover is shiny, and the pages have no pencil marks on them. Boy, is Luke excited! Have you ever borrowed a book from your teacher or the library that is not like the one Luke just got?

Luke has decided that he better follow some rules about taking care of books. Then, when he gives his book back to his teacher in the spring, it will still be in good shape.

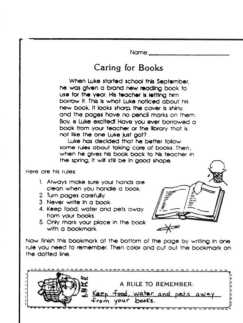

Here are his rules:

1. Always make sure your hands are clean when you handle a book.
2. Turn pages carefully.
3. Never write in a book.
4. Keep food, water and pets away from your books.
5. Only mark your place in the book with a bookmark.

Now finish this bookmark at the bottom of the page by writing in one rule you need to remember. Then color and cut out the bookmark on the dotted line.

A RULE TO REMEMBER:
Keep food, water and pets away from your books.

Page 26

Parts of a Book

Info needs Luke to help him understand some of the important parts of a book.

Spine – One of the first parts of a book you will see is the spine of a book. On the spine you will usually find Title, Author, Call Numbers and the Publishing Company.

Call Numbers – These numbers on the spine of the book will help you find the book in the library.

Title Page – This is the first page in most books. On this page you will find the Title, Author and Publishing Company.

Table of Contents – This is usually the second page in a book. On this page you will find the names of all the chapters in the book and the page numbers.

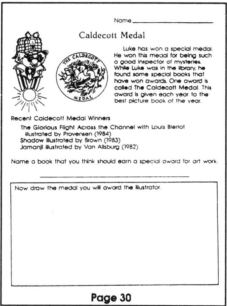

Fill in the blanks

1. You can find the title of a book on the title page and on the s_pine_.
2. The spine will have a _call_ number.
3. The Table of Contents will list each _chapter_.
4. The Publishing Company is listed on the spine and the _title_ page.
5. To count the chapters look at the _table_ of _contents_.

To solve my riddle, fill in the blanks. I know with your help Info will say thanks. He gets mixed up, each time he starts. Make it clear to him, all the important _parts_.

Page 27

Publishers and Authors

A Publisher is a company that prints books.

An Author is a person who writes books.

Most of the time the Publisher and Author of the book are listed on the spine of the book and the title page.

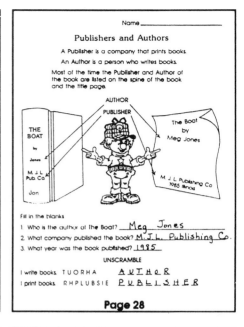

Fill in the blanks

1. Who is the author of the Boat? _Meg Jones_
2. What company published the book? _M.J.L. Publishing Co._
3. What year was the book published? _1985_

UNSCRAMBLE

I write books TUORHA _AUTHOR_

I print books RHPLUBSIE _PUBLISHER_

Page 28

Illustrator

Do you like to draw pictures? If you do, then someday you may become an illustrator of books. An illustrator is a person who draws pictures to go with stories. Just like the author makes the book come alive, the illustrator also makes the book come alive. If you like pictures in a book, remember the illustrator's name and watch for other books that he has illustrated.

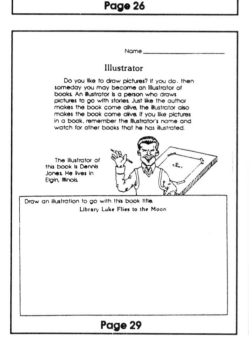

The illustrator of this book is Dennis Jones. He lives in Elgin, Illinois.

Draw an illustration to go with this book title.
Library Luke Flies to the Moon

Page 29

Caldecott Medal

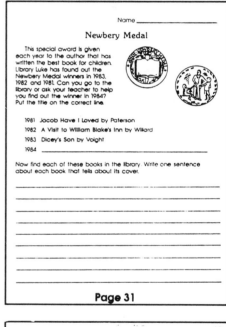

Luke has won a special medal. He won this medal for being such a good inspector of mysteries. While Luke was in the library, he found some special books that have won awards. One award is called The Caldecott Medal. This award is given each year to the best picture book of the year.

Recent Caldecott Medal Winners

The Glorious Flight Across the Channel with Louis Bleriot illustrated by Provensen (1984)
Shadow illustrated by Brown (1983)
Jamanji illustrated by Van Allsburg (1982)

Name a book that you think should earn a special award for art work.

Now draw the medal you will award the illustrator.

Page 30

Newbery Medal

This special award is given each year to the author that has written the best book for children. Library Luke has found out the Newbery Medal winners in 1983, 1982 and 1981. Can you go to the library or ask your teacher to help you find out the winner in 1984? Put the title on the correct line.

1981 Jacob Have I Loved by Paterson

1982 A Visit to William Blake's Inn by Willard

1983 Dicey's Son by Voight

1984 _____

Now find each of these books in the library. Write one sentence about each book that tells about its cover.

_____
_____
_____
_____
_____
_____
_____
_____
_____

Page 31

ABC Order

When putting words in ABC order, look at the first letters of the word. Sometimes the first letters in two words are the same. To decide which should come first, look at the second letter of the word.

EXAMPLE: The book Ramona the Brave by Beverly Cleary would be placed on the shelf before the book Pinocchio by Carlo Collodi because the letter l in Cleary comes before the letter o in Collodi in the alphabet.

Color me by putting the color words in ABC order and following the directions.

orange yellow blue purple red black green brown

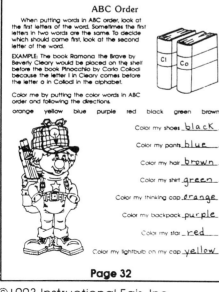

Color my shoes _black_

Color my pants _blue_

Color my hair _brown_

Color my shirt _green_

Color my thinking cap _orange_

Color my backpack _purple_

Color my star _red_

Color my lightbulb on my cap _yellow_

Page 32

ABC Order

Luke found out that he had to be pretty good at his ABC order if he wanted to find books in the library. To practice, he took his special equipment and placed it in boxes in ABC order.

Help Luke by cutting out the pictures and pasting them in the correct boxes.

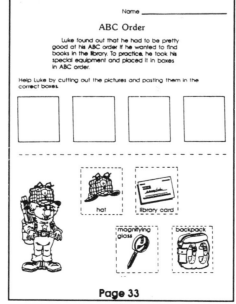

hat   library card

magnifying glass   backpack

Page 33

ABC Order

Put these author's last names in ABC order and find out what Info's favorite fiction book is. Then write the title of Info's favorite book at the bottom of the page.

1. _Alcott_
2. _Bailey_
3. _Caudill_
4. _Day_
and
5. _Enright_
6. _Freschet_
7. _Gaer_
8. _Hunt_
9. _Potter_
10. _Sendak_
11. _Smith_
12. _Yep_

AUTHORS

Carolyn Bailey
Ruth Smith
Laurence Yep
Irene Hunt
Maurice Sendak
Berniece Freschet
Beatrix Potter
Joseph Gaer
Elizabeth Enright
Cecil Lewis Day
Rebecca Caudill
Louisa May Alcott

Lady and the Tramp

Page 34

Fiction Books

Name

Luke and Info would like you to meet another one of their friends. His name is Fiction Finch. He is a bird. He is not an ordinary bird. He wears glasses. A real bird would not wear glasses. He is make-believe. That is why his name is Fiction Finch.

A Fiction Book is make-believe too. So, to help you remember what fiction means, think of Fiction Finch and his make-believe glasses.

You can find fiction books in the library in ABC order using the last name of the author.

Help Fiction Finch put these books in the order you would find them on the shelf of the library. Draw a line from each position to the book title.

Peter Pan by Barrie — 1st
The Borrowers by Norton — 2nd
Winnie-the-Pooh by Milne — 3rd
Fairy Tales by Anderson — 4th
Ralph Mouse by Cleary — 5th
Charlotte's Web by White — 6th
The Cat in the Hat by Seuss — 7th
The Biggest Bear by Ward — 8th
A Christmas Carol by Dickens — 9th
Tom Sawyer by Twain — 10th

Page 35

Non-Fiction Books

Info, Luke and Fiction Finch are going to bake a cake for their favorite librarian who helps them at the library. They need a book that will show them how to bake cakes. "How to" books are also called Non-Fiction. They are not make-believe, they are true.

Circle the book titles that are Non-Fiction.

The Cat in the Hat   Treasure Island
(Building a Doghouse)   The Ugly Duckling
(History of Baseball)   (Where the Wild Things Are)
(How to Make Doll Clothes) Alice in Wonderland
Peter Rabbit   The Incredible Journey
(Animals in the Jungle)   (Abe Lincoln)

Now use your crayons to decorate Luke's cake!

Page 36

Dewey Decimal System

A long time ago a librarian named Dewey invented a way to number books in a library so that they can easily be found.

Luke and Info use the Dewey Decimal System to help them find their favorite books. They learned that books about the same kinds of subjects have the same call numbers on the spines.

To find a Non-Fiction book in the library you use the Dewey Decimal System.

Luke has listed a few of his favorite subjects to look up. He has also listed the call numbers for each subject.

Science – call numbers 500 to 599
Pets – call numbers 600 to 699
Sports – call numbers 700 to 799

Write the correct call numbers next to each book title.

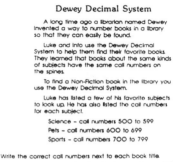

Feeding Your Dog by Owens __600__ to __699__
Lions in Africa by Downs __500__ to __599__
Game of Football by Bond __700__ to __799__
Sports and Games by Kieth __700__ to __799__
Baseball by Siebert and Vogel __700__ to __799__
Here Come the Dolphins by Goudey __500__ to __599__
Canada Geese by Scott __500__ to __599__
In the Days of the Dinosaurs by Andrews __500__ to __599__

Page 37

Picture Books

Each night before Info goes to bed, he likes Luke to read him a story. His favorite kind of books are called picture books because they have a lot of pictures. To find these in the library, Luke uses the Dewey Decimal System. On the picture books Mr. Dewey put a letter E and then the first three letters of the author's last name. On the shelves these books are then put in ABC order.

Here is one of Info's favorite books.

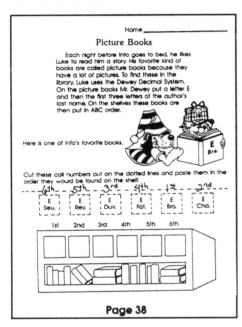

Cut these call numbers out on the dotted lines and paste them in the order they would be found on the shelf.

6th   5th   3rd   4th   1st   2nd

| E Seu. | E Rey. | E Duv. | E Fat. | E Bra. | E Cha. |

1st   2nd   3rd   4th   5th   6th

Page 38

Biography

Did you know that Thomas Edison invented the electric lightbulb? Michael Jackson used to sing with his brothers. Do you know how many brothers he sang with?

Library Luke learned about these two famous people when he read their biographies. A biography is a book that tells about the life of a famous person. Luke discovered that biographies are in the library in a special order. Each biography will have the number 92 and the first three letters of the famous person's last name.

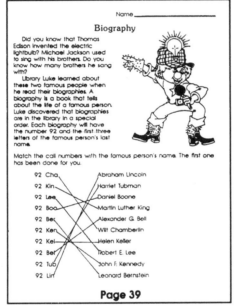

Match the call numbers with the famous person's name. The first one has been done for you.

92 Cha   Abraham Lincoln
92 Kin   Harriet Tubman
92 Lee   Daniel Boone
92 Boo   Martin Luther King
92 Bel   Alexander G. Bell
92 Ken   Wilt Chamberlin
92 Kel   Helen Keller
92 Bel   Robert E. Lee
92 Tub   John F. Kennedy
92 Lin   Leonard Bernstein

Page 39

Poetry

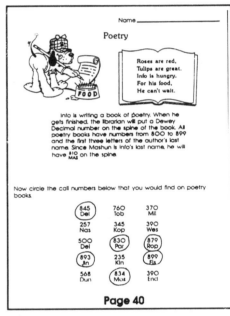

Roses are red,
Tulips are great.
Info is hungry.
For his food,
He can't wait.

Info is writing a book of poetry. When he gets finished, the librarian will put a Dewey Decimal number on the spine of the book. All poetry books have numbers from 800 to 899 and the first three letters of the author's last name. Since Mashun is Info's last name, he will have 810 Mas on the spine.

Now circle the call numbers below that you would find on poetry books.

(845 Del)   760 Tob   370 Mil
257 Nas   345 Kop   390 Wes
500 Del   (830 Par) (879 Rop)
(893 Jin)   235 Kin   (899 Fla)
568 Dun   (834 Mos) 390 End

Page 40

Cut and Paste Review

Luke has to answer these questions about the library. Will you help Luke? Cut the words out at the bottom of the page and paste them in the correct sentences.

1. The __Caldecott Medal__ is given to the best picture book each year.

2. An __Author__ is someone who writes a book.

3. Call numbers are listed on the __spine__ of the book.

4. Books about make-believe people are called __Fiction__.

5. The person that draws pictures for books is called an __Illustrator__.

6. The best story written each year is given an award called the __Newbery Medal__.

7. Call numbers were invented by __Dewey__.

8. Books about famous people are called __Biographies__.

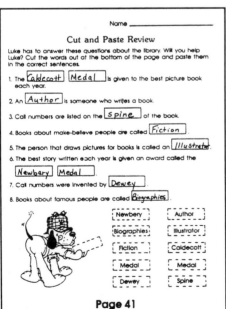

Newbery	Author
Biographies	Illustrator
Fiction	Caldecott
Medal	Medal
Dewey	Spine

Page 41

Crossword Review

Help Info work the crossword puzzle and discover what is under his jacket.

DOWN
1. Books about famous people are called what?
3. Make-believe books are called what?
4. How should you mark your place in a book?

ACROSS
2. Where are the call numbers written?
3. Which is last in ABC order: fat, fox, frog or fish?
5. Who writes books?

Page 42

Word Search Review

Info and Luke have been busy trying to find answers to the six questions below. They had them all figured out, then Info slipped and his paw knocked over the board with the letters on it. Now they are all mixed together! Find the answers to the questions and circle the correct words.

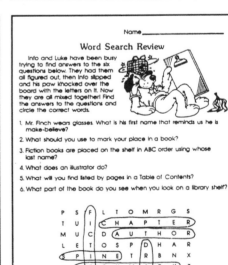

1. Mr. Finch wears glasses. What is his first name that reminds us he is make-believe?

2. What should you use to mark your place in a book?

3. Fiction books are placed on the shelf in ABC order using whose last name?

4. What does an illustrator do?

5. What will you find listed by pages in a Table of Contents?

6. What part of the book do you see when you look on a library shelf?

```
P  S  F  L  T  O  M  R  G  S
T  U  I  C  H  A  P  T  E  R
M  U  C  D  A  U  T  H  O  R
L  E  T  O  S  P  D  H  A  R
S  P  I  N  E  T  R  B  N  X
L  B  O  O  K  M  A  R  K  Z
M  W  N  Q  A  T  W  T  D  C
```

Page 43

IF5071 Library and Reference Skills